Mashiach ben Yoseph
משיח בן יוסף

Elhanan ben Avraham

Netivyah Bible Instruction Ministry

NETIVYAH
P.O. Box 8043
Jerusalem, 91080
ISRAEL

NETIVYAH U.S.A.
P.O. Box 1387
Mt. Juliet, TN 37121
U.S.A.

netivyah@netivyah.org.il
www.netivyah.org

ISBN (978-0-9818730-1-5)

Mashiach ben Yoseph,
by Elhanan ben Avraham

Printed in Israel

Mashiach
ben Yoseph

משיח בן יוסף

Elhanan ben Avraham

"The Torah was given in the language of men,"[1] in order that they might hear and understand. The achievements of mankind, especially in our time, have been outstanding, including the elevation of himself to heights above the laws of gravity, even into outer space. From such an elevated position he has been able to view the planet which contains all his history and sentiment and note from above that humankind itself is less visible than dust on an orange.

The Torah, on the other hand, was handed down to give men a view from the highest mountain in the highest range, as it were. From that high peak may be seen from whence he has come, where he stands at present, and choices he has regarding his future. The view is so magnificent that one may see beyond the evidence collected by the limited means of the senses and the reason dependent on them, into the realm of motive and origin, where all may be seen in the detail, and the detail is the reflection of all. As it is written: *"In your light we shall see light"* (Psalm/Tehillim 36:10).

As a tree is dependent on its root and cannot be separated from it, so each history given us in the Torah is foundational regarding future events and their meanings. As the Divine Hand was incorporated in the recording of the events, so it was not given for the end of entertainment, i.e., as an end in itself, but for instruction and edification, viable and pertinent to all generations.

I would like here to consider the Torah account of Yoseph Ha-Tzadik (Joseph), the "dreamer of dreams," and his brothers, the children of Israel. Perhaps, with G-d's help, we will see in light of the words and movements of those people in relation to one another, an even greater light, pertinent even to ourselves in our day.

I will call the story of Yoseph a love story, even though it is based on hatred, jealousy, and crime perpetrated by brothers against their own brother. I say a love story, for it is a wonderful picture of the working of G-d's love, as contrasted to the frailties and treacheries in the efforts of even the best of men.

I   Babylonian Talmud. Nedarim 3a.

By way of introducing this theme of "Mashiach ben Yoseph," allow me to quote the sages of the Talmud, "All the Prophets prophesied only of the days of the Messiah."[II] Moshe Rabeinu (Moses), who recorded these events of Yoseph's life, and who in fact brought the remains of Yoseph up out of *Mitzrayim* (Egypt), is considered in Judaism to be Israel's greatest prophet. If there is truth in the above, then is it not possible that we might learn something of the promised Messiah of Israel from the story of Yoseph? The Rabbis of Israel have also deduced, in that the writings of the Prophets give such a contrasting picture of Mashiach (rejected and slain vs. succeeding and reigning as king), that there are to be, in fact, two messiahs. One is to be "ben David" (the son of David) and the other "ben Yoseph" (the son of Yoseph). In the twelfth chapter of the Prophet Zechariah it is written, *"And I will pour out on the House of David and on the inhabitants of Jerusalem the spirit of grace and supplication, so that they will look on me whom they have pierced, and they will mourn for him as one mourns for an only son, and they will weep bitterly over him, like the bitter weeping over a first-born."* To this the Rabbis respond, "This is Mashiach ben Yoseph, who is to be slain."[III] But why is there reference at all to Yoseph, or to a "son" of Yoseph? It is to this question that I wish to address myself.

When Ya'akov Avinu (Jacob) was about to die, he gathered his sons around him and said, *"Gather yourselves together that I may tell you that which shall befall you in the end of days,"* (Genesis/B'resheet 49:1). The Hebrew for "the end of days" is acharit hayamim (אחרית הימים), the same form used in the Scriptures to refer to the latter days, the Day of the L-rd, the coming of Mashiach. Ya'akov then prophesied over each of his sons. Over Yoseph he said, *"Yoseph is a fruitful bough, even a fruitful bough by a well, whose branches run over the wall; the archers have sorely grieved him, and shot at him, and hated him, but his bow abode in strength, and the arms of his hands were made strong by the shepherd, the stone of Israel; even by the G-d of thy father, who shall help thee, and by the Almighty, who shall bless thee with blessings of heaven above, blessings of the deep that lieth under, blessings of the breasts, and of the womb; the blessings of thy father have prevailed above the blessings of*

II   Babylonian Talmud. Berachot 34b.

III   Babylonian Talmud. Sukkah 52/ Yalkut Shemoni.

my progenitors unto the utmost bound of the everlasting hills: they shall be on the head of Yoseph, and on the crown of the head of him who was separate from his brethren. " Was this amazing prophecy referring only to the remaining years of Yoseph, the son of Ya'akov? Do the prophetic words reach through time and generations to a later "son of Yoseph?" Has there been any figure in Jewish history to whom the "blueprint" dynamics of the life of Yoseph might point? The same question could equally be addressed to the final prophetic blessing made by Moshe concerning Yoseph (already long deceased) just prior to his own passing (D'varim/Deuteronomy 33:13-17).

Of course, any parable, prophecy, or parabolic allusion is not the same as the actuality to which it points, just as looking at a reflection in a mirror is not the same as looking directly into a face, nor is seeing a picture the same as experiencing the event of which the picture was made. Words themselves are as limited as the "exit" sign in a theatre which itself cannot be walked through, though the door to which it points its reader can be. So I pray that you, reader, will bring to this work, and to the Scriptures cited herein, the open eyes of your heart, and the open ears of your understanding.

Let us examine for a moment the meaning of the Hebrew word ben (בן) or son. The word may refer to an actual physical seed, or it may more specifically refer to one who is typologically in the character of another, whether he is or is not the actual physical offspring. It can refer to one who is a derivative of, or a disciple of another. It can refer to one who is a member or participant, such as *ben brit* (son of the covenant), or *bar mitzvah* (*bar* is the Aramaic equivalent of the Hebrew word *ben*).

The story of Yoseph ben Ya'akov begins with chapter 37 of B'resheet (Genesis). The form I will use in our discussion will be to examine this account chapter by chapter, at the same time comparing a parallel account of the life of another son of Avraham and Ya'akov, an Israeli Jewish rabbi of the First Century CE, who has had the most profound effect on the history of individuals and nations since that time. The ancient text I will cite for the account will be one written in the First Century CE Land of Israel, predominantly by Israeli Jewish contemporaries of the rabbi. The text is known commonly as the Brit Hadasha (New Covenant, New Testament). The rabbi was known in his day, in the Land of Israel, as

7

Yeshua ben Yoseph from Natzeret (Luke 4:22, John/Yohanan 1:45 and 6:42), the English derivative from the Greek being Jesus, son of Joseph, from Nazareth. I believe that as we examine the accounts of these two lives, side by side, we will discover striking parallels that I trust will not be without interest.

To begin with, there are statements made by Rav Yeshua that call to mind the Talmudic reference quoted earlier ("All of the Prophets prophesied only of the days of the Messiah"). *"These are my words which I spoke while I was still with you, that all things which are written about me in the Torah of Moshe and the Nevi'im (Prophets) and the Tehilim (Psalms) must be fulfilled"* (Luke 24:44). *"You search the Scriptures, because you think that in them you have eternal life; and it is these that bear witness of me"* (Yohanan 5:39). These are bold statements indeed for a son of Israel to make, and yet it is recorded that this one born in Beit Lehem (Bethlehem) from the tribe of Yehuda (Judah) and of the House of David, raised by Yoseph the carpenter and Miriam (Mary) his wife, did make them. Let us now turn to the ancient texts to see for ourselves if there may or may not be, in fact, some validity to such claims. (I would ask the reader to read along in the B'resheet/Genesis text.)

B'resheet 37:2 - The account very quickly enters into the dynamics of the relationships between Yoseph, his father, and his brothers, which were to embroil them in conflict. We see already a special relationship between the father and this one son, even as he brings a "bad report" about his brothers back to his father. Yeshua of Nazareth in several discussions with his brethren, the children of Israel, brought before them the issue of their *het* (sin): *"Those of the P'rushim (Pharisees) who were with him heard these things, and said to him, 'We are not blind too, are we?' Yeshua said to them, 'If you were blind, you would have no sin; but since you say, "We see," your sin remains"'* (Yohanan 9:40-41); and, *"If I had not come and spoken to them they would not have sin, but now they have no excuse for their sin"* (Yohanan 15:22). Yeshua also said. *"But whoever shall deny me before men, I will also deny him before my Father who is in Heaven"* (Matthew/Matatyahu 10:33). At the age of twelve, Yeshua declared to Yoseph and Miriam, when they finally found him in discussion in the Temple in Jerusalem, *"Did you not know that I had to* *be about the affairs of my Father?"* (Luke 2:49). These words and acts of both Yoseph and Yeshua could not be, and indeed were not, received by their brethren without eliciting a strong reaction.

37:3 - *"Israel loved Yoseph more than all his sons."* In the Torah (D'varim/Deuteronomy 14:1), we are told that the G-d of Israel has many sons: *"You are the sons of the L-rd your G-d."* In Matt. 3:17 and 17:5, it is reported that the same

The L-rd pronounced, *"This is my beloved son, hear him."* Again, the picture is of one favored of his Father. In B'resheet 22:2, we see that G-d tells Avraham, *"Take please now your son, your only son, whom you love, Itzhak (Isaac), and go to the land of Moriah, and offer him there as a burnt offering..."* At the time of that event Avraham already had a son born to him from his own seed: Ishmael. Therefore the idea of an "only son" here speaks of one who is chosen for a unique purpose, the only one of his kind, one through whom the covenant would be established (B'resheet 17:18-21). Yoseph was the son of Ya'akov's wife, Rachel, who had died and was buried by Beit Lehem, which is where Yeshua was born (Matt. 2:1).

37:4 - The fact that Yoseph was favored over his brothers by their father caused envy and jealousy to turn to hatred, and they could not speak well of him, nor address him with shalom. It could be said that they hated him without due cause (sinat hinam -שנאת חינם) Tehillim/Psalm 69:4), to which Yeshua referred regarding the response He received from some of the religious Jews, *"But this comes to pass that the word might be fulfilled that is written in their Torah, 'They hated me without a cause.'"* (Yohanan 15:25). The Rabbis have also declared that G-d allowed Jerusalem and the Temple to be destroyed in the First Century due to Sinat hinam.[IV] The same dynamic may be observed in the accounts of other brothers in the Torah: Cain and Hevel (Abel), as G-d had accepted Hevel's offering and was thus hated, to the point of murder, by Cain; Itzhak and Ishmael; Ya'akov and Esav; and later King Sha'ul and David. In each case, the elder persecuted the younger who had been selected by G-d for His purposes, (*"The elder shall serve the younger,"* B'resheet

IV   Babylonian Talmud. Yoma 9b.

25:23). Indeed, the majority of Jewish religious authorities, both in the First Century and now, cannot seem to bring themselves to speak well of Yeshua of Nazareth (ולא יכלו דברו בשלום *"They hated him, and could not speak peaceably unto him"*).

37:5-10 - Yoseph recounted his dreams to his brothers, and they *"hated him even more."* Yet the dreams he had received were in fact prophetic, not of his own fabrication, but given him by G-d, as we shall see as the account unfolds. At several points, Yeshua made equally bold announcements before Israel: *"Behold, there is here greater than Shlomo (Solomon)"* (Luke 11:31); *"But I say to you, there is here greater than the Temple"* (Matt. 12:6); *"In order that all may honor the son, even as they honor the Father"* (Yohanan 5:23); and Yeshua said before the Sanhedrin, *"...hereafter you shall see the son of man sitting at the right hand of Power, and coming on the clouds of heaven"* (Matt. 26:64), for which His elder brethren mocked, beat, spit at, and pronounced Him deserving of death.

37:11 - *"And his brothers were jealous of him."* Jealousy also stirred the religious authorities, as Pilate noted of Yeshua, *"For he was aware that the chief cohanim had delivered him up because of envy"* (Mark 15:10).

37:12-17 - Yoseph was sent by his father to his brothers, the children of Israel who were tending sheep in Sh'chem. Yeshua said, *"I have been sent only to the lost sheep of the house of Israel"* (Matt. 15:24), and *"... the Father has sent me"* (Yohanan 5:36).

37:18 - His brothers saw him from afar, and before he came close, plotted to kill him. To this day, Yeshua is seen from a distance by the children of Israel through a fog of prejudice and misunderstanding, through the sins of an idolatrous religious system which misused the name "Jesus," even attempting to erase his Jewishness. At that name, the Jew, for the most part, thinks negatively, linking it with the sufferings of the centuries, wishing to "kill" even the memory of it, that it might not come close to them to be objectively examined (as the acronym "Yeshu" which is the common pronunciation of his name in Hebrew, is intended by some to mean "may his name and memory be erased.")

37:19-20 - They mocked Yoseph and plotted to kill him. In Matt. 27:41, it is written, *"In the same way the chief cohanim (priests), along with the sof'rim (scribes) and z'kenim (elders), were mocking him and saying, 'He saved others, he cannot save himself; he is the king of Israel, let him now come down from the execution stake and we shall believe in him.'"* (c.f. Yohanan 8:39-59). We also find in Matt. 26:3-4, *"Then the chief cohen and the z'kenim of the people were gathered together in the court of the cohen who was called Caipha, and they plotted together to seize Yeshua by stealth, and kill him."*

37:21 - Reuven rose to Yoseph's defense. In Yohanan 7:51, we see the *cohanim* and *p'rushim* gathered in a plot to condemn Yeshua, and one of them, Nakdimon, arises in his defense, *"Our Torah does not judge a man unless it first hears from him and knows what he is doing, does it?"*

37:23 - They seized Yoseph and stripped him of his tunic still with the intent to destroy him. It is interesting that the account in the Brit Hadasha (Yohanan 19:23-24) describes the taking of Yeshua's garments, emphasizing the seamless, woven tunic of one piece, stripped from Him before His execution.

37:24-25 - They threw Yoseph into a pit, and they sat down to eat a meal. The time of Yeshua's arrest and imprisonment was *Pesach*, when Israel reclines to eat the *Seder Pesach* (Passover meal).

37:25-30 - Here we have the picture of Yehuda, one of the twelve, suggesting the selling of their brother for monetary gain, even as Yehuda (Judas) Ish Kiriot, one of the twelve talmidim (disciples) of Yeshua, sold him to the religious authorities. In both cases, this led to them being turned over to the goyim (Gentiles): Yoseph to the Egyptians, Yeshua to the Romans. Yeshua prophesied of Himself, *"And the son of man will be betrayed unto the chief cohanim and sof'rim, and they will condemn him to death, and will deliver him up to the Gentiles..."* (Matt. 20:18-19).

In both cases, the intended sellers of their brother were unable to retain the desired money, the Midianites stealing Yoseph before they could sell him, and in Matt. 27:37, *"Then when Yehuda, who had betrayed him, saw that he had been condemned, he felt remorse and returned the thirty pieces of silver to the chief cohanim and z'kenim, saying, 'I have sinned by betraying innocent blood' and he threw the pieces of silver into the sanctuary and departed.... And the chief cohanim took the silver and said, 'It is not lawful to put them into the treasury since it is the price of blood.' And they took council, and bought with them the potter's field to bury strangers in."* In the prophecy of Zechariah (11:13), it is written, *"Then the L-rd said to me, 'Throw it to the potter, that magnificent price at which I was valued by them.' So I took the thirty shekels of silver and threw them to the potter in the house of the L-rd."* This sum was the value of a slave gored by an ox (Shmot/Exodus 21:32).

37:31 - They slaughtered a male goat in Yoseph's stead, dipping his tunic in its blood. Though this occurred well before the *mitzvot* of the Torah were given, we have here a picture reminiscent of the goat offered as a *korban* (sacrifice) for sin (Vayikra/Leviticus 16:15), which Rashi described as "A life for a life." Vayikra 17:11 tells us, *"For the life of the flesh is in the blood, and I have given it to you upon the altar to make atonement for your souls, for it is the blood by reason of the life that makes atonement."* There is also here a *remez* (clue or hint) of a further dynamic of Yom Kippur, that of the second goat, the scapegoat (*azazel* which was to carry the sins of Israel into the wilderness) in the sending away of innocent Yoseph. The Prophet Yeshayahu (Isaiah) in chapter 53 speaks of one who was *"separate from his brethren,"* who *"Was despised and rejected of men, a man of pains and acquainted with grief, and like one from whom men hide their face, he was despised and we (Israel) did not esteem him. Surely our sickness he himself bore, and our pains he carried; yet we ourselves esteemed him stricken, smitten of G-d, and afflicted. But he was wounded for our transgressions, he was crushed for our iniquities, the chastening for our shalom fell upon him, and by his scourging are we healed. All of us like sheep have gone astray, each of us has turned to his own way, but the L-rd has caused the iniquity of us all to fall on him. He was oppressed and he was afflicted, yet he did not* *open his mouth; like a lamb that is led to the slaughter, and like a sheep that is silent before its shearers, so he did not open his mouth"* (3-7). (It is noteworthy that in this portion of the account of Yoseph, it is not recorded that Yoseph uttered a single word). *"But the L-rd was pleased to crush him, putting him to grief; if he would render himself as a guilt offering he will see his seed, he will prolong his days, and the desire of the L-rd will succeed by his hand. As a result of the anguish of his soul he will see it and be satisfied; by his knowledge the Righteous One, My servant, will justify many, and he will bear their iniquities. Therefore I will allot him a portion with the great, and he will divide the booty with the strong, because he poured himself out unto death, and was numbered with the transgressors; yet he himself bore the sin of many, and interceded for the transgressors"* (10-12). The Talmud Bavli, Sanhedrin 98b, refers to this passage as speaking of the Mashiach, as does the Targum Yonaton, Midrash Ruth Raba ("Melech ha-Mashiach"), and the Mahzor of Yom Kippur, Musaph ("Az milifney B'resheet"). In the Brit Hadasha (Matt. 20:28), Yeshua said, *"The son of man did not come to be served, but to serve, and to give his life a ransom for many,"* and (Matt. 26:28) *"For this is my blood of the covenant, which is to be shed on behalf of many for forgiveness of sins."* In Yohanan 1:29, it is said of Yeshua, *"Behold the lamb of G-d who takes away the sin of the world."*

37:32-35 - It was reported to Ya'akov/Israel that Yoseph was dead, and he was to remain with that belief for many years, until a much later revelation, when he would again see him. Yeshua has been considered dead and separate from the House of Israel for almost two millennia. Yeshua spoke a number of parables referring to a distant journey and a long passage of time, *"For the Kingdom of heaven is as a man traveling into a far country, who called his own servants, and delivered unto them his goods. ... Now after a long time the master of those servants came and settled accounts with them"* (Matt. 25:14-19); *"For the son of man is as a man taking a far journey..."* (Mark 13:34). Luke 17:24-30 says, *"For just as the lightning, when it flashes out of one part of the sky, shines to the other part of the sky, so will the son of man be in his day. But first he must suffer many things and be rejected of this generation. And just as it happened in the days of Noah, so it shall be in the days of* *the son of man.... It will be just the same on the day that the son of man is revealed."* Matthew 23:38-39 says, *"Behold your house is being left unto you desolate. For I say to you, from now on you shall not see me until you say, 'Blessed is he who comes in the name of the L-rd.'"*

37:36 - Both Yoseph and Yeshua were delivered to the *goyim*.

Chapter 38 - This chapter is a breaking away from the account of Yoseph and a turning of attention to Yehuda, who has played, and will continue to play, a key role in the fate of Yoseph. In that our intention is to examine the account of Yoseph, we will deal only briefly with this chapter on Yehuda. This chapter essentially leads us to the birth of Peretz ("breach"), from whose line would come King David, and Zarah ("he has risen"), the sons of Yehuda and Tamar. In the name Peretz, we have a *remez* regarding the later prophecy found in the Book of Micha (Micah) 2:12-13, which speaks of one called "the Breaker" (*poretz*) who would open the way for the remnant of Israel to "break forth." It reads thus: *"I will surely assemble all of you, Ya'akov; I will surely gather the remnant of Israel. I will put them together like sheep in a fold; like a flock in the midst of its pasture they will be noisy with men. The breaker has gone up before them, they break out, pass through the gate and go out by it, and their king goes on before them, and the L-rd at their head."* This passage is reminiscent of Pesach and of *yetziat Mitzrayim* (the Exodus from Egypt) under Moshe, but is of course a later work, prophesying a later, yet not dissimilar, event.[V] In Matt. 11:12-13, Yeshua said, *"And from the days of Yohanan ha Matbil (John the Immerser) until now the kingdom of heaven is taken by strength, and the strong take it by force."* His reference almost certainly is to the "breaking forth" in the prophecy of Micha of those with the full heart's desire to follow their King (Mashiach) who would break open the way before them, (*"I am the way, the truth, and the life; no man comes to the Father but through me"*- Yohanan 14:6). Yohanan 10:4-9 describes opening the gate under the leadership of the L-rd: *"When he puts forth all his own, he goes before them, and the sheep follow him because they know his voice... Truly, truly I say to you, I am the gate of the sheep... I am the gate; if anyone enters through me, he shall be*

V   See Seder Eliahu Rabbah p. 82 for an interesting *midrash* on this passage.

saved, and shall go in and out and find pasture." In Yohanan 13:36, it is recorded, *"Shimon Caipha said to him, 'Adoni, where are you going?' Yeshua answered, 'Where I go, you cannot follow me now; but you shall follow later.'"* This He said referring to His imminent crucifixion, and the profound significance of what was to occur by it. This occurred at Pesach according to the Gospels and the Babylonian Talmud Sanhedrin 43a.

I will not attempt here to explore the possible significance of Tamar's waiting for Shelah to come of age, and the prophecy of Ya'akov over Yehuda in chapter 49:10 of B'resheet, *"The scepter shall not depart from Yehuda, nor the ruler's staff from between his feet, until Shiloh comes."*

Chapter - 39:1-6 Yoseph was brought down to Egypt. Egypt (*Mitzrayim*) in the Torah stands as the antithesis of the Promised Land, *Eretz Israel*. It is a land of little water and plentiful sand, filled with *avoda zara* (false religion and idolatry); it is an oppressive regime and the house of bondage. It is from here that G-d was to deliver His people and bring them back to the land that He had promised to their fathers, "a land flowing with milk and honey," and where they were to learn to serve the Living G-d in truth by His Torah. They were to be "brought up" from the Land of Egypt, to go up (to make *aliyah*) to the land promised to Avraham Avinu. *Aliyah* is the same word used today for immigration to Israel. They were not to go "back down" to Egypt (Isaiah 31:1). In Yohanan 6:38, Yeshua declares, *"For I came down from heaven not to do my own will, but the will of him that sent me."* According to His words, He had left His Father's house and the glory (*kavod*) therein, to seek out "the lost sheep of the House of Israel" (Yohanan 14:2, 17:5). In the First Century, though *Am Israel* was in the land promised to them, they were still under the oppressive hand of the pagan Roman Empire and occupied by the Roman army. Religious leadership in Jerusalem was no longer truly established according to the Torah, but with those willing to compromise with the Roman authorities. The evident corruption in the religious system was stated in the records of the Jewish sect of Qumran (Dead Sea Scrolls). It was to this background that Yeshua came and stated, *"If you continue in my word, then are you my disciples indeed, and you shall know the truth, and the truth shall set you free."* To this the reply came that they are Avraham's seed and are in bondage to no man. *"Yeshua answered them, 'Truly, truly I say unto you, whosoever commits sin is the slave of sin. And the slave will not abide in the house forever: but the son will abide forever. If the son therefore shall set you free, you shall be free indeed"'* (Yohanan 8:31-36). It is written of Yoseph in Mitzrayim, *"That the L-rd was with him, and that the L-rd made all that he did to prosper in his hand."* This describes a relatively short period that Yoseph was a servant doing many good works in Potiphar's household, before his arrest. It is also written of Yeshua, concerning the three years before His arrest, *"All they that had any sick with various diseases brought them unto him; and he laid his hands on every one of them and healed them"* (Luke 4:40); and, *"Go your way and tell Yohanan what things you have seen and heard, how that the blind see, the lame walk, the lepers are cleansed, the deaf hear, the dead are raised, to the poor good tidings are announced"* (Luke 7:22, Isaiah 29:18-19). Yeshua also announced, *"The son of man came not to be served, but to serve..."* (Matt. 20:28).

39:7-19 - Yoseph was tempted by Potiphar's wife, which he was able to overcome, resisting a series of opportunities, unwilling to compromise and to "sin against G-d." In chapter 4:1-11 of Matitiyahu is the account of Yeshua's encounter with Ha-Satan (accuser, tempter), who tempted Him to compromise and break the commands of G-d, which Yeshua resisted on every point.

39:20 - For his moral and spiritual integrity and refusal to compromise, Yoseph was falsely accused and cast into prison. Again, I wish to note that there is no record here of Yoseph opening his mouth in his own defense before his accusers. It is recorded in Mark 14:55-61 that many false witnesses were brought to the trial of Yeshua, and that He spoke nothing in His own defense, other than answering in the affirmative when asked by the *Cohen Gadol* as to whether He was the Mashiach. In Matt. 27:12-14, we find, *"And when he was accused of the chief cohanim and z'kenim, he answered nothing. Then Pilatus said unto him, 'Do you not hear how many things they witness against you?' And he answered him not a word, insomuch that the governor marveled greatly."* The above is reminiscent of the prophecy of Yeshayahu (53:7-8). *"He was oppressed,* *and he was afflicted, yet he opened not his mouth: he was brought as a lamb to the slaughter, and as a sheep before her shearers is dumb, so he opened not his mouth. He was taken from prison and from judgment, and who will declare his generation?"* and, 53:12, *"He was reckoned among the transgressors."* Yeshua said, *"For I say unto you that this that is written must yet be accomplished in me. 'And he was reckoned among the transgressors:' for the things concerning me have an end"* (Luke 22:37, Yeshayahu 53:12).

39:21-23 - The L-rd was with Yoseph in prison, and the prisoners were given into his hand. "And whatever he did, the L-rd made it to prosper." This is the reference in Yeshayahu (53:10), *"Yet it pleased the L-rd to bruise him; He has put him to grief ... and the desire of the L-rd shall prosper in his hand."* Yeshua was executed and His body placed in the tomb. In the same passage of the Yeshayahu prophesy (53:9), it is written, *"And he made his grave with the wicked, and with the rich in his death, because he had done no violence, neither was any deceit in his mouth."* Shimon Caipha (Peter) has written concerning Yeshua, *"For Mashiach also has once suffered for sins, the just for the unjust, that he might bring us to G-d, being put to death in the flesh, but brought to life by the Spirit, by which he went and proclaimed unto the spirits in prison, which before were disobedient, when once the patience of G-d waited in the days of Noah, while the ark was being prepared, wherein few, that is, eight souls were saved by water"* (2 Peter 3:18-20). The prophecy of Yeshayahu (61:1) reads, *"The spirit of the L-rd God is upon me, for He has anointed me to proclaim good tidings unto the humble, He has sent me to bind up the brokenhearted, to proclaim liberty to the captives, and the opening of the prison to them that are bound."* This, along with another passage from the same prophet, Yeshua read in the *beit knesset* (synagogue) at the end of which He declared, *"This day is this scripture fulfilled in your ears"* (Luke 4:17-29). In the Revelation of Yohanan (1:18), Yeshua said, *"I ... have the keys of hell and death."*

Chapter 40:1-22 - Here Yoseph, as interpreter of dreams, was able to see, not by the sight of his eyes, but discerning the judgment of G-d concerning who shall live and who shall die. Yeshayahu 11:1-4 reads,

"And there shall come forth a rod out of the stem of Ishai, and a branch shall grow out of his roots. And the spirit of the L-rd shall rest upon him, the spirit of wisdom and understanding, the spirit of council and might, the spirit of knowledge and the fear of the L-rd and shall make him of quick understanding in the fear of the L-rd: and he shall not judge after the sight of his eyes, neither reprove after the hearing of his ears: but with righteousness shall he judge the poor, and reprove with equity for the humble of the earth, and he shall smite the earth with the rod of his mouth, and with the breath of his lips shall he slay the wicked." "Judge not according to the sight of your eyes, but judge righteous judgment," Yeshua taught (Yohanan 7:24), and, *"And yet if I judge, my judgment is true: for I am not alone, but I and the Father that sent me"* (Yohanan 8:16). Shimon Caipha said of Yeshua, *"And he commanded us to proclaim unto the people and to testify that it is he which was ordained of G-d to be judge of the living and the dead. To him give all the Prophets witness"* (Acts of the Shlichim/Apostles 10:42-43). All of the accounts reporting of Yeshua's arrest tell of the presentation by the Romans of Bar Abba and Yeshua before the crowds, that by their choice one would live and one die- a reflection of this account of the butler and the baker.

40:23 - The chief butler did not honor Yoseph's request, but forgot him when he was released, leaving Yoseph imprisoned. Again we see the picture of one rejected and abandoned, though he is righteous and correct in his judgments. Shimon Caipha denied knowing Yeshua three times the night of Yeshua's arrest (Matt. 26:69-75). It is also written of his talmidim at the time of His arrest, *"And they all forsook him and fled"* (Mark 14:50).

Chapter 41 - This chapter gives us the picture of a Hebrew who is able to bring solution to an unsolvable problem, to open a way before kings and wise men of the nations who were unable to find a way. Here is the prophecy of Yeshayahu (52:13-15), *"Behold, my servant shall deal prudently, he shall be exalted and extolled, and be very high. As many were astonished at thee, his appearance was so marred more than any man, and his form more than the sons of men: So shall he sprinkle many nations; kings shall shut their mouths at him: for that which had not been* *told them shall they see, and that which they had not heard they shall consider."*

41:14 - The highest power in *Mitzrayim* sent and called Yoseph hastily from out of the pit, the same word used to describe the hole which his brothers threw him into; also the same word used in the *Nevi'im* and the *Tehillim* for "the grave." In chapter 6:1-2 of the Prophet Hosea it is written, *"Come and let us return unto the L-rd: for He has torn, and He will heal us, He has smitten and He will bind us up. After two days He will revive us, in the third day He will raise us up, and we shall live in His sight."* The Brit Hadasha account describes that on the third day after the execution, the Most High revived Yeshua of Nazareth from the dead, and brought Him forth from the tomb. *"He is not here, but is risen: remember how he told you when he was yet in the Galil, saying, 'The son of man must be delivered into the hands of sinful men, and be crucified, and the third day rise again'"* (Luke 24:6-7). Yoseph *"shaved himself and changed his clothes, and came in unto Pharaoh,"* is a *remez* to the messianic prophecy of *Avdi Tzemach* ("My servant the Branch") in Zechariah 3, *"And he showed me Yehoshua the Cohen Gadol standing before the malach (angel) of the L-rd, and Ha-Satan standing at his right hand to accuse him. And the L-rd said unto HaSatan, 'The L-rd rebuke you, Ha-Satan, even the L-rd which has chosen Yerushalayim rebuke you: is not this a brand plucked out of the fire?'"* (In Luke 10:18, Yeshua said, *"I beheld Ha-Satan as lightning fall from heaven").+24*

In Zechariah 3:1-8 it says, *"Now Yehoshua was clothed with filthy garments, and stood before the malach. And he answered and spoke unto those that stood before him, saying, 'Take away the filthy garments from him.' And unto him he said, 'Behold, I have caused your iniquity (עֲוֹן) to pass from you, and I will clothe you with a change of clothing,' [c.f. Yeshayahu 53:6, speaking of the Servant of the L-rd, "And the L-rd has laid on him the iniquity of us all" (הפגיע בו את עון כלנו)]. And he said, 'Let them set a pure miter upon his head.' So they set a pure miter upon his head, and clothed him with garments. And the malach of the L-rd stood by. And the malach of the L-rd testified unto Yehoshua, saying, 'Thus says the L-rd of Hosts, if you will walk in my ways, and if you will keep my charge, then shall you also judge my house, and shall also keep my courts, and I will give you places to walk among these that stand by. Hear now, Yehoshua the Cohen Gadol, you, and your friends that sit before you: for they are a sign: for behold, I will bring forth my servant, the Branch'"* (c.f. Yeramiahu/Jeremiah 33:14-16). It is described in Matt. 17:1-2, *"And after six days Yeshua took Shimon Caipha, Ya'akov, and Yohanan his brother, and brought them up to a high mountain apart, and he was transfigured before them: and his face did shine as the sun, and his clothes as white was the light"* (Yeshayahu 61:10 says, *"For he has clothed me with the garments of salvation, he has covered me with the robe of righteousness"*).

41:15-16 - *"And Yoseph answered Pharoah, saying, 'It is not in me; G-d shall give Pharoah an answer of peace.'"* Yeshua said, *"The son can do nothing of himself, but what he sees the Father do: for what things so ever he does, these also do the son likewise. For the Father loves the son, and shows him all things that he does: and he will show him greater works than these, that you may marvel"* (Yohanan 5:19-20). Yoseph and Yeshua claimed to speak for G-d: *"The word which you hear is not mine, but the Father's which sent me"* (Yohanan 14:24).

41:17-36 - Yoseph, "the dreamer of dreams," again correctly interprets dreams, now doing that which the magicians and wise men could not. According to Jewish sources, the Mashiach is to give correct interpretation to Torah,[VI] which is "to fulfill" the Torah. In Matt. 5:17, Yeshua said, *"Think not that I come to destroy the Torah or the Nevi'im, I am not come to destroy, but to fulfill."* The Mashiach was to unlock the mysteries of the Torah and the Prophets. An event is described in Yeshayahu 29:9-14, *"For the L-rd has poured out upon you the spirit of deep sleep, and has closed your eyes: the prophets and your rulers, the seers has he covered. And the vision of all is become unto you as the words of a book that is sealed, which men deliver to one that is learned saying, 'Read this, I plead:' and he says, 'I cannot, for it is sealed;' and the book is delivered to him that is not learned, saying, 'Read this, I plead;' and he says, 'I am not learned.' Wherefore the L-rd said, 'For as much as this people draw near to me with their mouth, and with*

VI   B'resheet Rabbah 98.9.

their lips do honor me, but have removed their heart far from me, for their fear toward me is taught by the commandments of men; therefore behold, I will proceed to do a marvelous work among this people, even a marvelous work and a wonder: for the wisdom of their wise men shall perish, and the understanding of their sages shall be hidden.'" Yeshua, in discussing the resurrection with the *Tzadukim* (Sadducees), said, *"You err, not knowing the Scriptures, nor the power of G-d"* (Matt. 22:29). Of the state of the *sof'rim* and *p'rushim* (Scribes and Pharisees), He said, *"you blind guides"* (Mat. 23:16).

41:37-38 - Here the Gentile king declared that the Spirit of G-d was in Yoseph, but had not his brothers, the children of Israel, mocked him for his visions? Much the same has occurred during the last two millennia, with many from among the goyim declaring that the Spirit of the L-rd is in Yeshua, while much the opposite has been said by our own people Israel. Yeshua had said *"The Spirit of the L-rd is upon me,"* but the *P'rushim* said, *"This fellow does not cast out sheddim (demons) but by Ba'al Zevuv, the prince of the sheddim"* (Matt. 12:24). Similarly it is written, *"Then answered the Jews, and said unto him, 'Do we not say well that you are a Samaritan, and there is a shedd within you?'"* (Yohanan 8:48).

41:39-41 - Yoseph, the insignificant servant, was brought forth from prison in obscurity and raised up above the heads of both the Gentiles and his own brethren, to sit at the right hand of the power of the king Pharoah. The king said to him, *"According unto your word shall all my people be ruled,"* giving him full authority. It may be seen here also, the one who lay in the confines of the tomb and death, utterly defeated from Israel's eyes, and from that of the Romans (the Egypt of its day), suddenly brought forth from obscurity and raised up from death, conquering the most unconquerable of all in resurrection and raised up to the right hand of the throne of power (*g'vurah*) of *HaShem HaMevurach*. Tehillim 110:1 states, *"The L-rd said unto my lord, Sit at my right hand, till I make your enemies your footstool"* (Yalkut interprets this as "King Messiah"). Yeshua stated in Matt. 28:18, *"All authority has been given unto me in heaven and on earth,"* and, *"Henceforth you shall see the son of man* *sitting at the right hand of power, and coming on the clouds of heaven"* (Matt. 26:64). The Prophet Daniel thus describes the Mashiach. (As interpreted by Rashi and Metzudat David, this is "Melech HaMashiach"). *"I saw in the night visions and behold, one like unto the son of man came with the clouds of heaven, and came to the Ancient of Days, and they brought him near before him. And there was given him dominion, and glory, and a kingdom, that all people, nations, and languages should serve him: his dominion is an everlasting dominion, which shall not pass away, and his kingdom that which shall not be destroyed"* (7:13-14). From the Talmud, we have described one called "Metatron" (i.e. one next to the throne), in the story of "Four entered paradise" and saw there one seated next to the throne of the Most High.[VII]

41:42 - Again here is the image of the changing of garments. Yoseph was adorned with the outer garments and symbols of Egyptian royalty - certainly styled from head to foot - in Gentile garb. He became totally unrecognizable to his Hebrew brothers. After the First Century CE, Yeshua was taken and, as it were, made "King of the Gentiles," wrapped in the garments of foreign custom, and in time even hidden under the heavy accoutrements of idolatrous religion, (which would turn His light to darkness), which essentially forgot that *"King of the Jews"* was written above the execution stake upon which He suffered death. All the above helped serve to blind the eyes of His own nation and brethren, Israel, who have even lost sight, to a high degree, of His being indeed a Jewish rabbi of our own.

41:43-44 - Yoseph had been called by the king himself to reign with him over all the land, giving Yoseph equal authority. They cried before Yoseph, "Bow the Knee." In Yohanan 5:23, Yeshua said, *"He who honors not the son, honors not the Father who sent him."* The King Messiah would reign over the Earth with G-d. *"It is a light thing that you should be my servant to raise up the tribes of Ya'akov, and to restore the preserved of Israel. I will also give you for a light to the Gentiles, that you may be my salvation unto the ends of the earth"* (Yeshayahu 49:6). *"Yet have I set my king upon my holy hill of Zion. I will declare the decree:*

VII   Babylonian Talmud. Hagiga 14-15.

The L-rd has said unto me, 'You are my son, this day have I begotten you. Ask of me, and I shall give you the nations for an inheritance, and the uttermost parts of the earth for your possession'" (Tehillim 2:6-8, which Yalkut and Metzudat David interpret as referring to Mashiach). Yoseph, rejected by the children of Israel, became king over *Mitzrayim*; Yeshua, officially rejected by Israel, became king over Gentiles.

41:45 - Yoseph received a new name, of the Gentiles, Tzaphnat-paneah. Yeshua received through translation the Greek name "Yesous," becoming "Jesus" in English and losing its original Hebrew meaning of "salvation" (Matt. 1:21). In the Revelation to Yohanan 3:12, Yeshua says, *"And I will write upon him my new name."* In Yeramiahu 23:5-6, the name of the "Branch" - Messiah - is to be "the L-rd our Righteousness" ('ה צדקנו). Yoseph married the daughter of the Gentile priest. Yeshua's "bride" (Rev. 19:7-9) would also be those Gentiles called out from and cleansed of idolatry, being taught of the G-d of Israel and His Torah *"Until the fullness of the Gentiles comes in"* (Sha'ul's letter to the Romans 11:25).

41:46 - Yoseph was thirty years old when he stood before Pharoah. This is the age according to the Torah (Bamidbar/Numbers 4:3) that a man may begin priestly service in the Tabernacle. Yeshua, when he began his works in Israel, was *"about thirty years old"* (Luke 3:23).

41:50-52 - Two sons were born to Yoseph, Menasha and Ephraim. When Ya'akov blessed the two children, he laid his right hand on the head of Ephraim, the younger, (again the reversal of roles with the firstborn), and declared that *"his seed shall become the fullness of the goyim"* (B'resheet 48:19). He also said that Yoseph's two sons were as his own two firstborn sons, Reuven and Shimon. Thus these two were later to become half-tribes, numbered among the twelve in the inheritance of the Land of Israel, causing the name of Yoseph to rest in a separate and unique position, further fulfilling Ya'akov's prophecy over him that he would be "separate from his brethren" (B'resheet 49:26). Yeshua chose twelve intimate *talmidim* according to the number of the tribes of Israel, Himself separate, the thirteenth.

41:55 - *"And Pharoah said unto all the Egyptians, 'Go unto Yoseph, what he says to you, do.'"* In D'varim/Deuteronomy 18:15 Moshe states, *"The L-rd your G-d will raise up unto you a prophet from amongst you, of your brethren, like unto me; unto him you shall hearken."* In 18 and 19 of the same chapter, the L-rd confirms, *"I will raise them up a prophet from among your brethren, like unto you, and I will put my words in his mouth, and he shall speak unto them all that I shall command him. And it shall come to pass, that whoever will not hearken unto my words which he shall speak in my name, I will require it of him."* (Later we shall see what the Talmud says regarding this passage). In the Brit Hadasha, the L-rd declares of Yeshua, *"This is my beloved son, in whom I am well pleased, hear him"* (Matt. 17:5). Yeshua also clarified, *"The words that I speak unto you I speak not of myself, but the Father that dwells in me..."* (Yohanan 14:10). In 5:46 of the same book, *"For had you believed Moshe, you would have believed me; for he wrote of me."*

41:56-57 - Yoseph was able, through the intercession of the L-rd's spirit of wisdom, understanding, council, knowledge, and the fear of the Lord (Yeshayahu 11:2) to save the land from starvation, from lack of bread. In Matatyahu 14:15-21, Yeshua blessed five loaves of bread and two fish, which were then passed out and fed over five thousand people. The Torah tells us, *"Man shall not live by bread alone, but by every word which proceeds from the mouth of G-d"* (D'varim 8:3). In the Book of Amos 8:11, it is prophesied, *"'Behold, the days come,' says the L-rd G-d, 'that I will send a famine in the land, not a famine of bread, nor a thirst for water, but of hearing the words of the L-rd.'"* In the days of Yeshua, it had been over four hundred years since a prophet of G-d had been in the Land, to bring forth His word. Malachi had been the last. The nations of the world at that time were immersed in all forms of idolatry. Yeshua told His disciples, *"But you will receive power after the Ruach Ha-kodesh (Holy Spirit) is come upon you: and you shall be witnesses unto me both in Jerusalem, and in all of Yehuda and Shomron (Samaria), and unto the uttermost part of the earth"* (Acts 1:8) and, *"Go therefore, and teach all nations..."* (Matt. 28:19). In Yeshayahu 55:2-3, it is written, *"Wherefore do you spend money for that which is not bread and you labor for that which does not satisfy? Listen diligently unto me and eat that which is* *good, and let your soul delight itself in fatness. Incline your ear, and come unto me: hear, and your soul shall live; and I will make an everlasting covenant with you, even the sure mercies of David."* Yeshua said, *"I am the bread of life: he that comes unto me shall never hunger. and he that believes in me shall never thirst"* (Yohanan 6:35). Thus Yeshua would save the land from spiritual starvation, and bring the knowledge of G-d to the goyim, to a starving world, who then, knowing the ways of life and death, could choose accordingly. So it is written in the Torah, *"I call heaven and earth this day against you, that I have set before you life and death, blessing and cursing: therefore choose life"* (D'varim 30:19).

Chapter 42 - The completely natural and essential phenomenon of hunger was used here to draw Israel out to *Mitzrayim,* toward the fulfilling of God's overall plans. Yet this speaks of a hunger of the spirit, perhaps unbeknownst to them at the time. In Matt. 5:6, Yeshua said, *"Ashrei (blessed) are they that hunger and thirst after righteousness..."* He also said, *"Truly, truly, I say unto you, Moshe gave you not that bread from heaven; but my Father gives you the true bread from heaven. For the bread of G-d is he which comes down from heaven, and gives life unto the world"* (Yohanan 6:32-33).

42:6 - Here is the eventual fulfillment of Yoseph's prophetic dream, after many years. Though the children of Israel did not know that they were bowing before their brother and would not have admitted to the fact, *"they worshipped him"* (וישתחוו לו אפיים ארצה). This is the same gesture of bowing down before kings or G-d. As in the case of King David's dedication of Shlomo in I Chronicles 29:20, *"And all the congregation blessed the L-rd G-d of their fathers, and bowed down their heads and worshipped the L-rd and the king"* (וישתחוו לה' ולמלך)

42:7 - *"And Yoseph knew his brethren, but they knew him not."* Yoseph did his best to maintain that distance of unrecognizing, being in full control of the situation, though his brothers were completely ignorant of the fact. In the Prophet Yechezkel/Ezekiel 39:23 it is written, *"And the nations shall know that the house of Israel went into captivity for their iniquity because they trespassed against me; therefore I hid my face from* *them, and gave them into the hand of their enemies....*" We are reminded again of Yeshua's words, "*You shall not see me again until you say, 'Blessed is he that comes in the name of the L-rd.'*" So it was to be that Yeshua's identity would be hidden from Israel, yet they would be known of Him, as it is written in I Yohanan 4:19, "*We love him because he first loved us,*" and in Shaul's words in Romans 5:8, "*But G-d commended his love toward us, in that while we were yet sinners, Mashiach died for us.*"

42:17-18 - Yoseph imprisoned his brothers for three days, on the third day calling them forth. This recalls the passage in Hoshea 6:2, "*After two days he will revive us: in the third day he will raise us up, and we will live in his presence.*" It is written that Yeshua was raised up, according to His word, on the third day, from death. In Yohanan 11:25, "*Yeshua said unto her, I am the resurrection, and the life...*"

42:21-22 - The brothers began to associate their predicament with what they had done to Yoseph, though they in no way perceived him. (There has been an awakening of interest of a positive sort in Yeshua among a number of Jewish writers and scholars, including Martin Buber and Rabbi Eliyahu Solevitchik, who for the most part have not recognized Him as the promised Messiah.)

42:23-24 - "*And they knew not that Yoseph understood them, for he spoke to them by an interpreter. And he turned himself about from them, and wept...*" Yoseph wept upon hearing his brothers' conversation, which he understood in Hebrew. In Luke 19:41-42, Yeshua was in Jerusalem, "*And when he was come near, he beheld the city, and wept over it, saying, 'If you had only known, in this your day, the things which belong unto your peace (shalom) but now they are hid from your eyes.'*" There is a parallel in that the earliest accounts of Yeshua's life were written in Hebrew, then translated to Greek and Latin and then most other languages, where much of the Hebrew depth and culture was lost, and became utterly foreign to the Jewish people.

42:25-34 - Yoseph indeed answered their supplications by supplying their needs, loading their donkeys with grain, and even returning their money in their sacks. This is a fine illustration of *hesed* (grace), that they would know that what they had obtained had not been either deserved or by their own earnings. Though many in Israel do not recognize the validity of the Torah, nor the portion in the Rambam's statement of faith regarding the coming of Mashiach, yet is HaShem faithful to His word, *"for his hesed endures forever."* It is written in the Prophet Yechezkel 36:22, regarding the regathering of Israel to the Land, *"Thus says the L-rd G-d, I do not this for your sakes, O house of Israel, but for my holy name's sake..."*

42:35-38 - Israel saw no good coming from this situation, but evil only, and fear. This was the deduction of the leaders in Jerusalem in the First Century CE, *"If we let him thus alone, all will believe on him, and the Romans shall come and take both our land and our nation"* (Yohanan 11:48). This condition also exists for the most part in Israel and the Jewish people today, regarding our relation to Yeshua and the Brit Hadasha.

Chapter 43:1-7 - Yoseph had told them, *"You shall not see my face, except your brother be with you."* He would eventually gather all of his brothers together before him, while his true identity was yet hidden from them. It is thus prophesied in Yechezkel chapter 39:28-29, *"Then shall they know that I am the L-rd their G-d, which caused them to be led into captivity among the nations and I have gathered them unto their own land, and have left none of them any more there. Neither will I hide my face any more from them: for I will pour out my spirit upon the house of Israel, declares the L-rd G-d."* The reader is given to understand that Yoseph knows more about the children of Israel than they know of him, as they are completely in the dark regarding him. Today the average Jew knows little or nothing of Yeshua of Nazareth, other than distortions and preconceptions.

43:11 - Offerings were to be given to this unknown "man," the same who had angered them when told that they would make obeisance to him. At that time, had they known that it was Yoseph to whom they were offering *mincha*, it would have been a mighty shock to them.

43:14 - Here Israel called for G-d's mercy in the situation, neither knowing nor understanding that Yoseph is in fact G-d's instrument of mercy. This, according to the Brit Hadasha account, is the exact parallel to the work of G-d in Yeshua toward Israel (see Sha'ul's letter to the Romans, chapter 11). *"For G-d has concluded them all in unbelief, that he might have mercy upon all."*

43:15-16 - This is the second time the brothers appeared before Yoseph, the king. He commands, *"Bring these men home, and slay, and make ready, for these men shall dine with me at noon."* In the period of the second national return to the Land of Israel (the first being from Egypt, the second from Babylon), which is the time of the Second Temple, Yeshua appeared to Israel, in fact dining with His brethren. In Luke 22:15, Yeshua says, *"How greatly have I desired to eat this Passover with you before I suffer."* In Yeshayahu 53:7, it is written, *"He was brought as a lamb to the slaughter"* This word for "slaughter" is the same Hebrew word used in Yoseph's command. As Yoseph fed his brothers, so Yeshua said, *"I am the bread of life: he that comes to me shall never hunger, and he that believes on me shall never thirst,"* (Yohanan 6:35).

43:18-35 - *"And the men were afraid, because they were brought into Yoseph's house."* The closer they came to Yoseph, the more uncomfortable they grew, in effect experiencing their transgression (as we shall see later), though not yet knowing why. Yeshua said, *"If I had not come and spoken unto them, they had not had sin, but now they have no cloak for their sin"* (Yohanan 15:22). Yeshua's ultimate function was to deal with the matter of sin: *"For this is my blood of the new covenant (brit hadasha), which is shed for many for the remission of sins"* (Matt. 26:28). In verse 23, the fact is here spoken that Yoseph's generosity, which put fear in their hearts, was the work of the G-d of Israel. Though his brethren had betrayed him and cast him out, yet did he repay them with goodness, in fact fulfilling Yeshua's teaching, *"But I say unto you, 'Love your enemies, bless them that curse you, do good to them that hate you...'"* (Matt. 5:44). In verse 18, we see that Yoseph's generosity has been interpreted as malicious, and as yet is Yeshua's kindness often spoken evil of amongst our people.

43:26-28 - *"And bowed themselves to him to the earth."* Again we see the literal fulfillment of Yoseph's dream, confirming the prophetic nature of it. It is written in the Revelation of Yohanan 5:12, *"Worthy is the Lamb that was slain to receive power and riches, and wisdom, and strength, and honor, and glory, and blessing."*

43:30-31 - We witness the depth of Yoseph's feeling, expressed in tears hidden from his gathered brothers, along with his identity. Yeshua wept over Jerusalem and said, *"O Jerusalem, Jerusalem, you that kills the prophets, and stones them which are sent unto you, how often would I have gathered your children together, even as a hen gathers her chicks under her wings, but you would not"* (Matt. 23:37).

43:34 - Yoseph fed his brothers in his own home. In Luke 22:30, Yeshua said, *"That you may eat and drink at my table in my kingdom..."*

Chapter 44:1-12 - Again Yoseph provides sustenance and returns their money, the picture of *hesed* (grace). This time, however, by design he will use another tactic to make them aware of that *hesed*. A false accusation is leveled against them as a means of drawing out the nature of their actual transgression: hardness of heart and unbelief, and hatred expressed those many years earlier. As G-d the righteous judge will not allow transgression to go unpunished at some point, so are the children of Israel taken in this trap, arrested, and hindered from returning to the Land of Israel. A parallel to this is the accusation often leveled at Jews: "Christ killers." As we shall see shortly, the betrayal and turning over of Yeshua to the Roman authorities for execution was not in the essence of crime, for His death was of Divine intention for the highest purpose. Yeshua said concerning His life: *"No man takes it from me, but I lay it down of myself"* (Yohanan 10:17-18). The transgression, according to the prophets, including Moshe, was hardness of heart, unbelief, and "hatred without a cause."

44:13-34 - Here the sons of Israel tear their garments in dismay as their worst fears come upon them, and all hope of success appears to be lost. The above principle is well illustrated in Yehuda's expression of his deep guilt (it is he who had wished to murder, and later sell, Yoseph), realizing that *"G-d has found out the iniquity of your servants."* He confessed, *"What shall we say unto my lord? What shall we speak, or how can we clear ourselves?"* We may recall the words of Yeshayahu 53:8, *"and who shall declare his generation?"* Here Yehuda brings forth to Yoseph his long harbored anguish of spirit for his crimes against Yoseph himself (as yet unrecognized) and the pain which this had caused to their father, wishing now to repent by laying down his own life for the sake of his younger brother Benyamin. It is noteworthy that the rejection of Yoseph had caused such profound grief to Israel, the father, as Yeshua's rejection has been the anguish of Israel. Yet it is in the return, the repentance, of Yehuda here that we see before us the prophecy, *"For the redeemer shall come to Zion, and unto them that turn from transgression in Ya'akov, declares the L-rd"* (Yeshayahu 59:20). (It is from his name Yehuda that we get the word *Yehudi,* or Jew). Yeshua declared, *"Greater love has no man than this, that a man lay down his life for his friends"* (Yohanan 15:13). At that moment, Yehuda in his desire to cover his own sin against Yoseph and his father by laying down his life for Benyamin did not understand that Yoseph's life had already been given to redeem not only Yehuda, but all his brothers and their families. This is much the same principle seen in the *Akeida,* that G-d himself provided a life in the place of Yitzhak's on the sacrificial altar. This is also seen in the sin sacrifices in the later temple system ("A life for a life").

Chapter 45:1-2 - It is Yehuda's broken-hearted confession that finally tears the curtain of separation, and their redeemer is revealed before their eyes. *"The sacrifices of G-d are a broken spirit. A broken and contrite heart, O G-d, you will not despise"* (Tehillim 51:17 or 51:19 in Hebrew). Here is the essence of *t'shuva shlemah* (perfect repentance). How deep is the feeling in the breast of Yoseph and the love for his brothers. He can no longer contain the feeling, and he cries aloud. The Gentiles hear the weeping, though he has sent them out, making this a private family matter. Is not the gathering of Israel back to the Land in our days, separating them from the nations, for a purpose? In Yechezkel 36:24-26 it is written, *"For I will take you from among the nations and gather you out of all the countries, and will bring you into your own land. Then will I sprinkle clean water upon you, and you shall be clean from all your filthiness, and from all your idols will I cleanse you. A new heart will I give you, and a new spirit will I put within you; and I will take away the stony heart out of your flesh, and I will give you a heart of flesh."* Yeremiahu, describing the gathering of Israel to her land, brings the prophecy, *'"Behold, the days come,' declares the L-rd, 'that I will make a new covenant (brit hadasha) with the house of Israel, and with the house of Yehuda, not according to the covenant that I made with their fathers in the day that I took them by the hand to bring them out of the land of Egypt, which my covenant they broke, although I was a husband unto them,' declares the L-rd. 'But this shall be the covenant that I will make with the house of Israel, after those days,' declares the L-rd, 'I will put my Torah in their inward parts, and write it in their hearts, and I will be their G-d, and they shall be*

31

my people. And they shall teach no more every man his neighbor, and every man his brother, saying, "Know the L-rd," for they shall all know me, from the least of them unto the greatest of them,' declares the L-rd, 'for I will forgive their iniquity, and I will remember their sin no more'" (31:31-34). By design it is in the third time that his brothers appear before Yoseph that he chooses to reveal his identity to them. Likewise, this today is the third national gathering from exile of the Jewish people back to the Land of Israel. As stated earlier, the first was from Egypt under Moshe, the second was the return from Babylon, and now the third is from all the nations of the world. The prophecy in Yeremiahu 16:14-15 states, *"'Therefore behold, the days come,' declares the L-rd, 'that it shall no more be said, "the L-rd lives, that brought up the children of Israel out of the land of Egypt;" but, "The L-rd lives, that brought up the children of Israel from the land of the north, and from all the lands where he has driven them." And I will bring them again into their land that I gave unto their fathers.'"* The intent here is to gather Israel together again to speak to them privately, in their own language. (Hebrew was not a spoken, living, language for most of two millennia, until the advent of Zionism).

45:3 - *"And Yoseph said unto his brethren, 'I am Yoseph; does my father yet live?' And his brethren could not answer him, for they were troubled at his presence."* Allow me to again refer here to the passage which the Rabbis state speaks of "Mashiach ben Yoseph," Zechariah 12:10-14. *"And I will pour upon the house of David, and upon the inhabitants of Jerusalem the spirit of grace and supplication; and they shall look upon me whom they have pierced, and they shall mourn for him as one mourns for his only son, and shall be in bitterness for him, as one that is in bitterness for his firstborn. In that day there shall be a great mourning in Jerusalem, as the mourning in Hadadrimon in the valley of Megiddon. And the land shall mourn, every family apart; the family of the house of David apart, and their wives apart; the family of the house of Natan apart, and their wives apart; the family of the house of Levi apart, and their wives apart; the family of Shimei apart, and their wives apart; all the families that remain, every family apart, and their wives apart."* Here is one presumed dead by Israel, torn by a wild beast, suddenly appearing alive in the most unexpected form, time, and place, asking if his father Israel lives, the answer which he already knows. In Matatyahu 24:30 Yeshua states, *"And then shall appear the sign of the son of man in heaven: and then shall all the tribes of the land mourn, and they shall see the son of man, coming in the clouds of heaven with power and great glory."* Yoseph's brothers cannot answer his question, for they are deeply troubled, as the tribes and families of Israel shall mourn, husbands and wives not able to look into each other's eyes or speak, as they behold the Mashiach ben Yoseph.

45:4-6 - Mourning is for a limited period of time, as Yoseph speaks kindly unto them, *"Please come unto me"* (גשו נא אלי). Yeshua said, *"Come unto me, you who are weary and heavy laden, and I will give you rest"* (Matt. 11:28). In another place, (Yohanan 5:40), He says, *"And you will not come unto me, that you might have life."* Yoseph tells them, *"I am Yoseph, your brother, whom you sold into Egypt."* He comforts his brothers with great love and tenderness, explaining that this was all the work of G-d for the salvation of their lives, (and of course of the lives of the Gentiles who would receive his council and teachings), literally, "to bring to life."

45:7 - *"And G-d sent me before you to preserve you a posterity in the earth, and to save your lives by a great deliverance."* Yoseph was G-d's tool used in fulfilling the promise to Avraham of making his seed a great nation (Gen. 12:2). In Yohanan 14:2-3, Yeshua's words are, *"In my Father's house are many dwellings... I go to prepare a place for you. And if I go and prepare a place for you, I will come again and receive you unto myself, that where I am, there you may be also."* He speaks here of His death and its special significance, that His provision would not be only a temporary one, as Yoseph had provided, nor a terrestrial sanctuary that time would change, but an eternal place of glory in the Kingdom of Heaven. Yoseph had gone before Israel as a shepherd before his flock, bringing them to food and water, even if his sheep were reluctant. *("Give ear, O Shepherd of Israel, you that leads Yoseph like a flock"*- Tehillim 80:1). Yeshua, who declared, *"I am sent only to the lost sheep of the house of Israel"* (Matt. 15:24), also said, *"I am the good shepherd: the good shepherd gives his life for the sheep ... No man takes it from me, but*

I lay it down of myself" (Yohanan 10:11, 18). Here is one unlike Yoseph, who has voluntarily taken the role of outcast for the salvation of the flock of Israel.

45:8 - Yoseph reiterates that it had all been the outworking of G-d and declares his lordship over the house of Pharoah and the land of Egypt. Yeshua said, *"All authority has been given to me in heaven and on earth"* (Matt. 28:18).

45:9 - Yoseph commands his brothers to tell Israel the good tidings, (which is the meaning of "gospel"), of their deliverance and that they must come to him to receive it. Yeshua commissioned His twelve disciples (and others) to declare the *b'sorah* (good news) to Israel, and to all nations (Mark 28:19).

45:10-13 - Yoseph tells them, *"You shall be near unto me,"* in the place he had prepared. Yeshua said, *"Father, I will that they also whom you have given me, be with me where I am, that they may behold my glory, which you have given me...."* (Yohanan 17:24). Yoseph said, *"And you shall tell my father of all my glory in Egypt, and all that you have seen."* In Matatyahu 11:4-5 Yeshua said, *"Go and tell Yohanan that which you hear and see; the blind receive their sight, the lame walk, the lepers are cleansed, the deaf hear, the dead are raised up, and the poor have good news brought to them."*

45:14-15 - This is one of the most touching moments in all of Bible history, as the children of Israel receive their brother and deliverer who had been hidden from their eyes, embracing each other with profound tears of joy. Such joy will be at the revelation of the Mashiach.

45:16 - The Gentiles heard of this and were pleased. In Tehillim 126:12 it is written, *"When the L-rd returned the captivity of Zion, we were like them that dream. Then was our mouth filled with laughter, and our tongue with singing. Then said they among the Gentiles, 'The L-rd has done great things for them.'"*

45:17-20 - With the suggestion and authority of the king Pharoah, Yoseph gathers his people together. In Matatyahu 24:31, Yeshua said, *"And he shall send his malachim with the sound of a great shofar, and they shall gather together his elect from the four winds, from one end of heaven to the other."* Moshe promised, *"If any of yours be driven out unto the outmost parts of heaven, from there will the L-rd your G-d gather you, and from there will he fetch you"* (D'varim 30:4).

45:21 - Upon this joyous occasion, Yoseph gave his people gifts. Sha'ul stated in the letter to the Ephesians 4:9, quoting Tehillim 68:18 (68:19 in Hebrew), *"You have ascended on high and returned the captivity and took gifts for men."* In Rev. 22:12, Yeshua says, *"And behold, I come quickly, and my reward is with me, to give every man according as his work shall be."*

45:22 - Yoseph gave his brothers new clothing. Yeshayahu 61:10 says, *"For he has clothed me with garments of salvation, wrapped me with a robe of righteousness."* In Revelation 6:11 we find, *"And white robes were given unto every one of them."*

45:24 - Yoseph told his brothers not to become angry at each other on the way. Yeshua told his disciples, *"Whoever is angry with his brother without cause shall be in danger of judgment,"* and *"Love one another"* (Matt. 5:22, Yohanan 13:34).

45:26 - The center of Yoseph's message to Ya'akov here was, "Yoseph is alive," but he did not believe them. Luke 24:11 describes how when it was first reported to Yeshua's eleven disciples that He was alive, *"They believed them not."* The Brit Hadasha's report that Yeshua is alive has been, for the most part, disbelieved by Israel. The prophecy of Yeshayahu 53 begins, *"Who has believed our report, and to whom has the arm of the L-rd been revealed?"*

45:27 - When Israel finally did believe the report, before actually seeing Yoseph, *"the spirit of Ya'akov their father revived,"* literally, "Ya'akov's spirit came back to life." Shaul states, regarding Israel's return and their relation to Yeshua, that it will be *"life from the dead"* (Romans 11:15).

Chapter 46 - Here we see the gathering of Israel to Yoseph in *Mitzrayim* for the purpose of making there "a great nation." In the prophesies of Yechezkel we see that the gathering of the Jewish people to King Messiah will, in fact, be in the Land of Israel for a similar purpose, *"For thus declares the L-rd G-d, 'Behold, I, even I, will both search my sheep, and seek them out. As a shepherd seeks out his flock in the day that he is among his sheep that are scattered, so will I seek out my sheep, and will deliver them out of all the places where they have been scattered in the cloudy and dark day. And I will bring them out from the people, and gather them from the countries, and will bring them to their own land, and feed them upon the mountains of Israel by the rivers, and in all the inhabited places of the country.... Therefore will I save my flock, and they shall no more be a prey, and I will judge between lamb and lamb. And I will set up one shepherd over them, and he shall feed them, even my servant David, he shall feed them, and he shall be their shepherd. And I the L-rd will be their G-d, and my servant David a prince among them; I the L-rd have spoken it'"* (Yechezkel 34:11-13, 22-24). In chapter 37:24-26 of the same prophet, it is written, *"And David my servant shall be king over them, and they shall all have one shepherd. They shall also walk in my judgments, and observe my statutes, and do them. And they shall dwell in the land that I have given unto Ya'akov my servant, wherein your fathers have dwelt, and they shall dwell therein, even they and their children, and their children's forever. And my servant David shall be their prince forever. Moreover I will make a covenant of peace with them; it shall be an everlasting covenant with them. And I will place them, and multiply them, and I will set my sanctuary in the midst of them forevermore."*

46:27 - There were seventy souls in the house of Ya'akov. Seventy, in Judaism, is the traditional number of the nations, probably coming from D'varim 32:8, *"When the Most High divided to the nations their inheritance, when he separated the sons of Adam, he set the bounds of the people according to the number of the children Israel."* The prophecy of

Yeshayahu 49:6 states, *"It is a light thing that you should be my servant to raise up the tribes of Ya'akov, and to restore the preserved of Israel. I will also give you for a light to the nations that you may be my salvation unto the end of the earth."* Yoseph was sent forth by G-d for the salvation from hunger of both the Gentiles and Israel. In Matt. 28:19, Yeshua said, *"Go therefore, and teach all nations."* The Hebrew letter ayin (ע) is the number seventy. This is the last letter in the name Yeshua (ישוע). Amongst the Jewish people for most of two millennia, the last letter of his name has been traditionally dropped, making "Yeshu" (ישו). Ayin (עין) is also the Hebrew word for "eye." In Sha'ul's letter to the Romans chapter 11:25-26, we find, *"that blindness in part is happened to Israel, until the fullness of the Gentiles be come in. And so all Israel shall be saved, as it is written, 'There shall come out of Zion the deliverer, and shall turn away ungodliness from Ya'akov; for this is my covenant unto them, when I shall take away their sins.'"* It is written in Yeshayahu 42:6-7, *"I the L-rd have called you in righteousness, and will hold your hand, and will keep you, and give you for a covenant of the people, for a light to the nations,* (לברית עם לאור גויים) *to open the blind eyes..."* In Luke 4:20-21, it is recorded that Yeshua read these words in the *beit knesset* (synagogue) after which *"The eyes of all them that were in the synagogue were fastened on him. And he began to say unto them, 'This day this scripture is fulfilled in your ears.'"* In numerous places it is recorded that Yeshua also healed the physically blind.

46:28 - Yehuda was sent first to direct Israel unto Yoseph in Goshen. This interplay between Yehuda and Yoseph, and the dynamic between them in the entire account, plus the prophecy given by Ya'akov over Yehuda (B'resheet 49:8-12), is a *remez* to the Mashiach ben Yoseph coming forth ultimately from tribe of Yehuda. The name Yehuda in Hebrew (יהודה) actually contains the four letters of the Tetragrammaton, or the name of the L-rd, plus one letter, "d" (ד), from which comes "David" (דוד). In D'varim 12:11 we find, *"Then there shall be a place which the L-rd your G-d shall choose to cause his name to dwell there."* The inheritance of the tribe of Yehuda, the Land of Yehuda, therefore actually does contain the name of the L-rd. David ("beloved") ben Ishai, from whose seed was to arise the "son of David," or "Mashiach ben David," was born from the tribe of Yehuda, in the Land of Yehuda, and in the town of Beit Lehem, all of which is true also of Yeshua (Luke 2:1-7; Matt. 2:1-6). In Micah 5:2, it is prophesied, *"But you, Beit Lehem Ephrata, though you be little among the thousands of Yehuda, yet out of you shall come forth unto me that is to be ruler in Israel, whose goings forth have been from old, from everlasting."* We read in Sh'mot 23:20-21, *"Behold, I send a malach before you, to keep you in the way, and to bring you into the place which I have prepared. Beware of him and obey his voice; provoke him not, for he will not pardon your transgression. For my name is in him."* In Yeremyahu 23:5-6 it, appears, *"'Behold, the days come,' declares the L-rd, 'that I will raise unto David a righteous Branch... and this is his name whereby he shall be called, "the L-rd (the tetragammaton) our righteousness (צדקנו 'ה).""'"* Is it not possible, therefore, that Mashiach ben Yoseph and Mashiach ben David, are in fact one and the same person, an individual in whom the Holy One, Blessed be He, has chosen to place His name?

46:29 - Israel embraces his son whom he thought was dead, after a long passage of time, with tears of joy. First we saw the reunion of the brothers, and now of the old father, with Yoseph. The coming together of Israel with her Mashiach will be the fulfillment of the dreams, visions, and hopes of our Fathers, indeed of all the prophets of Israel. Yeshua said, *"...When you shall see Avraham, Itzhak, and Ya'akov and all the prophets, in the malchut haElohim (kingdom of G-d)..."* (Luke 13:28), and in Yohanan 8:56, He said, *"Your father Avraham rejoiced to see my day; and he saw it, and was glad."*

46:30 - *"And Israel said unto Yoseph, 'Now Let me die, because I have seen your face, because you are yet alive.'"* In Luke 2:28-32, we see the aging Shimon ha-Tzadik in the Temple at the time of the *brit mila / circumcision* of Yeshua, when he took the infant up in his arms and said, *"L-rd, now let your servant depart in peace according to your word, for my eyes have seen your salvation, which you have prepared before the face of all people; a light to illumine the Gentiles, and the glory of your people Israel."* Luke 24:5-6 reports of Yeshua at the tomb in which He had been placed, *"Why do you seek the living among the dead? He is not* *here, but is risen."*

Chapter 47:1-12 - This portion deals with the situation of Israel as shepherds and their flocks. Throughout the Tenach, the people of Israel are referred to as sheep and as the flock of the L-rd, as in Psalm 79:13, *"So we your people and sheep of your pasture will give you thanks forever,"* and Yeremiahu 50:6, *"My people have been lost sheep."* Likewise, G-d himself is called a shepherd, *"The L-rd is my shepherd"* (Psalm 23:1) and *"Give ear, O Shepherd of Israel"* (Psalm 80:1). As a good shepherd leads his flock to grazing, G-d, through Yoseph, has led Israel from famine to fullness and rest, as we read in 47:12, *"And Yoseph nourished his father and his brethren and all his father's household with bread, according to their families."* In the Brit Hadasha, Yeshua is described, like Israel, as both lamb and shepherd: *"Behold the lamb of G-d, who takes away the sin of the world"* (Yohanan 1:29) and *"They overcame him by the blood of the Lamb"* (Rev. 12:11) and *"I am the good shepherd; I lay down my life for the sheep"* (Yohanan 10:14-15). In Matatyahu 26:31, Yeshua refers to the prophecy of Zechariah 13:7 as speaking of Himself, *"'Awake, O sword, against my shepherd, and against the man who is my fellow,' declares the L-rd of Hosts. 'Strike the shepherd, and the sheep shall be scattered...'"* After this, follows the description of the *galut*, the dispersion of Israel. The salvation wrought through Yoseph, fulfilling G-d's promise to Avraham in Gen. 15:12-16, was in preparation of the greater deliverance of Pesach, over 400 years later. Pesach is one of the central *hagim* (festivals) of Judaism, to which even Shabbat points, and is remembered in the *tefillin*.

In Sh'mot 12:21, Israel was commanded to, *"Take a lamb according to your families, and kill the pesach,"* putting its blood upon the doorpost of each house as a sign (as we still put the mezuzah on our doorpost), the obedience to which would deliver them from death and the "house of bondage." *("And when I see the blood I will pass over you, and the plague shall not be upon you to destroy you"*- Sh'mot 12:13). It is evident here that central to the Passover, indeed, the *pesach* itself, is *the lamb*. It was at the Seder of Pesach that Yeshua said, at the blessing of the cup of salvation, *"This cup is the new covenant in my blood, which is poured out for you"* (Luke 22:20). It was also at Pesach that Yeshua was slain. Sha'ul writes, *"For Mashiach, our Pesach, is sacrificed for us"* (I Corinthians 5:7). In the Akeida, G-d provided a lamb (Gen. 22:7-8) as a *korban* in the place of Itzhak. Itzhak had carried the wood for his own death, to which Yalkut Shimoni remarked, "Like a man who carries his own cross." G-d's instrument by which the Pesach would be wrought was Moshe Rabeinu, who was raised up as a shepherd for forty years in the desert. He prophesied, *"the L-rd your G-d will raise up unto you a prophet from the midst of you, of your brethren, like unto me; unto him you shall listen."* It is written in Bamidbar Raba 11:3, "As it was with the first redeemer, so shall it be with the last redeemer" (כגואל ראשון כך גואל אחרון). When Moshe first came to his people Israel, was he not rejected, with them saying to him, *"Who has made you a prince and a judge over us?"* (Sh'mot 2:14). In Luke 2:14, Yeshua repeated these same words in a similar situation, referring to Himself and to His role and state before Israel. After this, did not Moshe disappear from the sight of Israel's eyes for many years? After this long absence, he would return as their redeemer. Another *remez* to this appears in the fact that Moshe ascended and descended Mount Sinai twice, disappearing for forty days, during which time Israel proved itself unready to receive the first covenant, in falling away with the golden calf. Because of this transgression, the plates of the covenant (לוחות הברית) were broken, and Moshe had to ascend and return a second time to complete the covenant. Yeshua has clearly spoken of His return a second time to fulfill all that which He had begun, to complete the covenant and all that which has been prophesied. This also appears in the prayer "Az m'lifney B'resheet" (אז מלפני בראשית) in the Yom Kippur prayer book

47:13-26 - This section describes the fulfillment of Yoseph's interpretations and of his councils. All had come to pass according to his words, and during the great famine, Yoseph had become the sole source for the region's food supply. By this, Yoseph succeeded in acquiring all the land for the king, and the people said to him, *"You have saved our lives, let us find grace in the sight of my lord, and we will be Pharoah's servants."* It should be noted that many years passed before Yoseph's words were proven true. Yeshua describes a time of tribulation to come upon the earth which would include famine, *"Immediately after the tribulation of those days... and then shall appear the sign of the son of* *man in heaven..."* (Matt. 24:29-30). In Matt. 25:31-32, He says, *"But when the son of man shall come in his glory, and all the malachim with him, then shall he sit on the throne of his glory. And before him shall be gathered all the nations..."* In the first letter to the Corinthians 15:24, Sha'ul writes of Yeshua, *"Then will come the end, when he shall have delivered up the Kingdom to G-d, even the Father, when he shall have put down all rule and all authority and power."*

Here I wish to move to chapter 50:15-21 of B'resheet, the time immediately following the passing of Ya'akov. It had been some seventeen years (47:28) since Yoseph had revealed himself to his brothers, when they came to ask his forgiveness, saying, *"Forgive, please the crime of your brothers, and their sin, for they did unto you evil; and now please forgive their crime..."* Yoseph, one of the most sensitive persons in all Scripture, wept when they spoke to him. His brothers fell down before him and said, as the Egyptians had, *"Behold we are your servants."* Yoseph then answered them, *"But as for you, you thought evil against me, but God meant it unto good, to bring to pass as it is this day, to save many people alive."* Yeshua said, from the cross upon which He was executed, *"Father, forgive them, for they know not what they do,"* (Luke 23:34) Though the children of Israel had been made aware of Yoseph's true identity, yet did a long time pass, seventeen years, before an open acknowledgement was made by them. It is written in the Prophet Hoshea 3:4-5, *"For the children of Israel will abide many days without a king, and without a prince, and without a zevach (sacrifice), and without an image, and without an ephod, and without t'raphim. Afterward shall the children of Israel return, and seek the L-rd their G-d, and David their king, and shall fear the L-rd and his goodness in the latter days (achrit hayamim.)"*

Allow me to conclude with a quote from the Midrash on Psalm 95:7.

"Rabbi Yehoshua ben Levi came upon Eliyahu (Elijah) standing at the entry to the cave of Rabbi Shimon ben Yohai. He said to Eliyahu, 'When will Mashiach come?'

He said: 'Go ask him.'

- 'And where is he to be found?'
- 'At the gates of Rome.'
- 'And what are his signs?'
- 'He is sitting among the beggars suffering from sores. They all remove and remake all their bandages at once, but he removes and remakes his one at a time, thinking: "Should I be required, I shall not be delayed."'

"Rabbi Yehoshua went there. He said to the Mashiach: 'Peace to you, my master and teacher.'

He said to him: 'Peace to you, son of Levi.'

He said: 'When will the Master come?'

He said: 'Today.'

"Rabbi Yehoshua went back to Eliyahu and said to him: 'He lied to me, for he said he would come today, and he has not come.'

Eliyahu said to him: 'Thus he said to you: "Today- if you would but hear his voice."'"

The same Psalm continues in verse 8, *"Harden not your heart..."* In Yohanan 10:27, Yeshua said, *"My sheep hear my voice..."*

Is there a conclusion to be drawn from all this? Is it conceivable that the words in Yeshayahu 53:6, *"All of us like sheep have gone astray"* are, in fact, true? I will leave this to the discretion of the reader. Allow me to add, however, that today, if we should hear the voice of a greater Yoseph, let us bless Him who said, *"Behold, I stand at the door and knock; if any man hear my voice and open the door, I will come in to him and will sup with him, and he with me"* (Rev. 3:20), by answering, *"Blessed is he that comes in the name of the L-rd"* (ברוך הבא בשם ה' -baruch haba b'shem Adonai).

"May our eyes behold your return unto Zion in mercy.
Blessed are you, O L-rd, who returns his presence unto Zion."[VIII]

(ותחזינה עינינו בשובך לציון ברחמים, ברוך אתה ה' המחזיר שכינתו לציון)

Jerusalem, Israel

VIII   This is a prayer appearing numerous times in the Siddur, the Jewish prayer book.